CORNHUSK, SILK, AND WISHBONES

A BOOK OF DOLLS

FROM AROUND THE WORLD

BY MICHELLE MARKEL

Houghton Mifflin Company Boston 2000

For Martin, with love

Copyright © 2000 by Michelle Markel

Pages 4, 10, 15, 34: courtesy of the Brooklyn Children's Museum.

Page 7: courtesy of the Museum of New Mexico Collections, in the Museum of International Folk Art, Santa Fe. Photo by Blair Clark.

Pages 8, 9, 13, 26, 31, 33, 38: courtesy of the Wenham Museum, Wenham, Massachusetts. Photos by Rob Huntley.

Page 14: courtesy of the British Museum.

Pages 16, 19, 22, 28: courtesy of the Rosalie Whyel Museum of Doll Art, Bellevue, Washington. Photos by Charles Backus.

Page 20: courtesy of the Museum of Northern Arizona Photo Archives (92C.60) (E843).

Page 21: courtesy of the Wenham Museum, Wenham, Massachusetts.

Page 25: courtesy of the Museum of the Confederacy, Richmond, Virginia. From *The Civil War: Spies, Scouts and Raiders.*
   Photo by Larry Sherer. Copyright © 1985 by Time-Life Books, Inc.

Page 27: courtesy of Basia Dziewanowska. Photo by Rob Huntley.

Page 32: courtesy of the Buffalo Bill Historical Center, Cody, Wyoming.

Page 37: courtesy of the Fowler Museum of Cultural History, UCLA. Photo by Denis J. Nervig.

Pages 39, 40: courtesy of the Girard Foundation Collection, Museum of International Folk Art, Museum of New Mexico, Santa Fe.
   Photos by Blair Clark.

Page 43: courtesy of the Natal Museum, Pietermaritzburg, South Africa.

www.hmco.com/trade

The text of this book is set in 10-point ITC Garamond 1.

Library of Congress Cataloging-in-Publication Data

Markel, Michelle.

Cornhusk, silk and wishbones: a book of dolls from around the world / Michelle Markel.

p.   cm.

Summary: Examines a variety of dolls throughout the world, discussing how they have been used at different times
and how they reflect the cultures that created them.

ISBN 0-618-05487-1

1. Dolls—Social aspects—Juvenile literature. 2. Dolls—Cross-cultural studies—Juvenile literature. [1. Dolls.] I. Title.

GN455.D64   M37   2000   688.7'221—dc21   99-089789

Printed in Singapore

TWP 10 9 8 7 6 5 4 3 2 1

INTRODUCTION

For centuries, people have created little objects shaped like themselves. There is something wondrous about them. They have a magic all their own. They inspire endless imaginings in the person to whom they belong. We call them dolls.

In our part of the world we know dolls as playthings, beloved companions, or perhaps precious objects to admire. But throughout the years, they have been used for many different reasons. In India, for example, they were once offered as sacrifices to gods. Long ago in Europe, before the spread of Christianity, Nativity figures were used to teach the story of the holy family. The Potawatomi and other Great Lakes Indians created dolls to make people fall in love with each other.

The doll makers of the world have been skilled craftsmen, loving relatives, caregivers, and determined children. They've found ways to make dolls and doll clothes out of everything from cornhusks and wishbones to fine silks and silver threads.

Dolls may look like the people who made them or like supernatural beings. Their bodies may be made of the jungle, the prairie, the desert, and may reveal what plants and animals lived there.

Let these dolls be messengers to you from other times and places. Discover what they have to say.

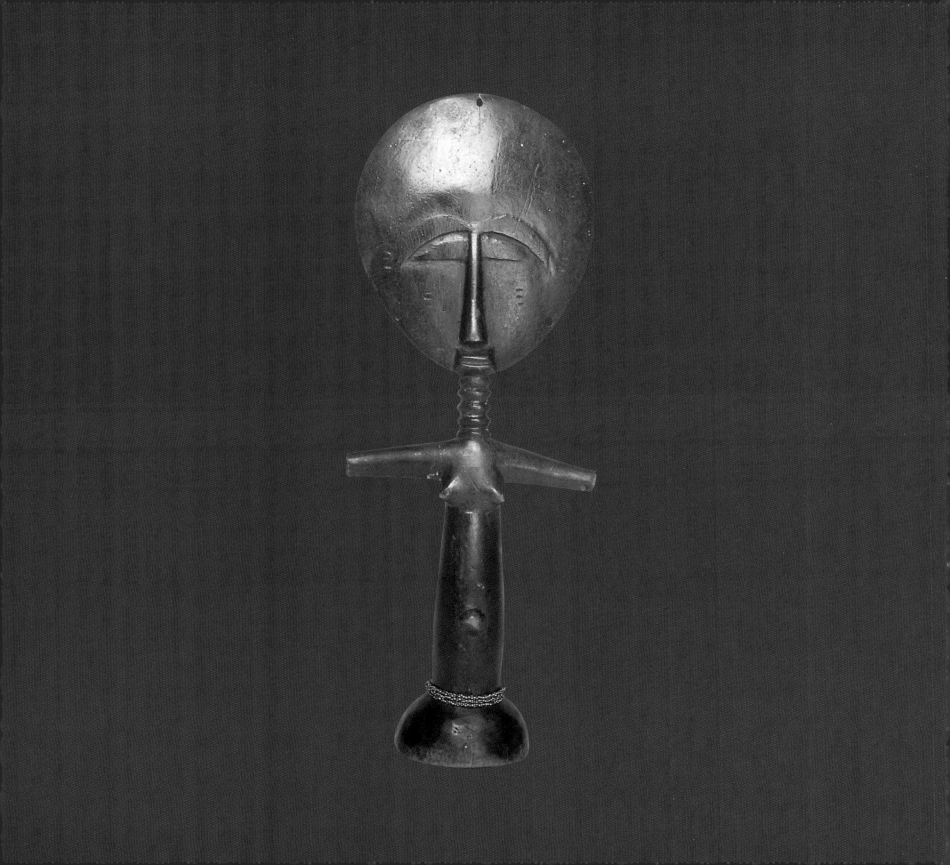

Akuaba (uh-KOO-uh-BAH) dolls are always girls. Their foreheads are high and wide, a sign of beauty to the Ashanti people of Africa. The dolls are named for a woman called Akua who the Ashanti believe lived long ago. Akua wanted a child very much but couldn't have one. A priest told her to get a baby carved from wood and to care for the doll as if it were real. Akua carried the wooden infant in a wrap on her back, fed her, gave her presents, and slept with her at night. In a little while, she indeed gave birth to a beautiful baby girl. Nowadays, if young women have trouble bearing children, they carry wooden dolls like Akua's on their backs.

AKUABA DOLL

From Ghana, c. 1900–1950

BREAD DOLLS

November 2 is All Soul's Day in Ecuador. On the morning of the holiday, children help their mothers make bread dolls. They shape balls of dough into small people and animals, guaguas de pan (GUAH-guahs day PAHN), then press on tiny decorations. In the past, the native people of Ecuador took the dolls, along with drinks and flowers, to the tombs of their loved ones. They believed the souls of the dead came to visit and should be welcomed with a ceremony. Today, Ecuadorans take bouquets to the cemetery and later have a family gathering. They serve the bread dolls with *colada morada,* a corn drink tinged purple with raspberry juice. A boy might search for his bread doll from the pile on the table. He'll turn the man over to see the name he carved, admire him one last time, then eat him up.

From Ecuador, 1985

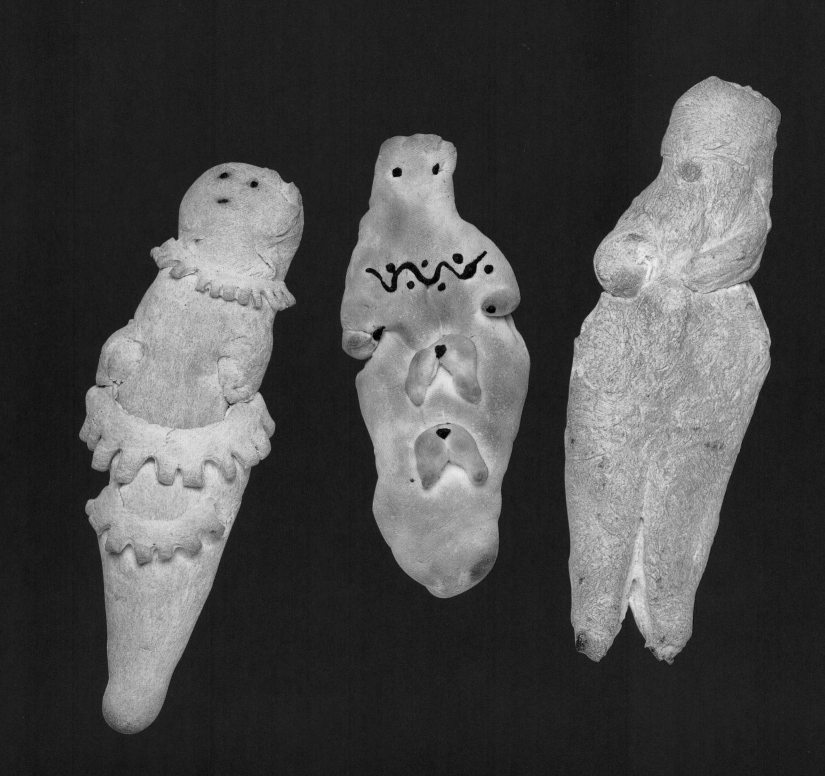

CORN DOLL

The early Americans didn't have lots of money, but they did have lots of corn. They used the cobs for kindling, the kernels for soup, bread, and pudding, the husks for rugs, baskets, mattresses—and for dolls. Some girls made entire families, using small sweet corn for babies and children and larger field corn for parents. Clothes and faces could be colored with the juice of vegetables or berries. In late summer, a girl might pick a fat ear of corn to make a lady. First she'd boil the husks to soften them; then she'd fold and tie the leaves into a little body, adding more to make a dress. She might use corn kernels for buttons and fresh corn silk for yellow hair. If the doll looked too plain, she could pick some wildflowers. When they dried, they'd be pretty on a hat.

From U.S., c. 1890

DAIRI-SAMA DOLLS

On the third day of the third month of the year, Japanese girls celebrate Hina Matsuri (hee-nah maht-soo-ree), Doll Festival Day. Their mothers spread a cloth over a stand with several shelves to make them an imperial court. The Dairi-Sama (die-ee-ree sah-mah), the emperor and empress, rule from the top shelf. Below them sit the ladies-in-waiting, musicians, ministers, and other members of the court. Mothers use this time to tell their daughters about the history of their country. They teach them how to serve the dolls food and drink. The girls wash and polish the tiny dishes that will be used. They plan the menu and go shopping for miniature versions of vegetables, fish, cakes, iced nuts, and other delicacies. On the day of the festival the girls prepare a meal and serve it to the Dairi-Sama and their court.

From Japan, c. 1900

ERE IBEJI

More twins are born to the Yoruba people of Nigeria than anywhere else in the world. When a twin dies, the mother has a wooden doll carved to take his or her place. She may adorn the Ere Ibeji (air-ee ee-BAY-jee) doll with camwood powder, blue dye, beaded necklaces, bracelets, or anklets. From then on, she treats it like the living twin. On the day he would have been honored as a twin by the village, she'll prepare a feast for the doll. She must do these things because the Yoruba believe that if twins are well treated, they'll bring good fortune, but if not they may cause sickness in, or even death, to the rest of the family. When the surviving twin grows up, he may care for the doll, or his family may give it to a woman called a "mother of twins." She makes sure the wooden children are fed, bathed, and put to bed, just as they expect.

From Nigeria, c. 1900–1950

These dolls have no moveable parts, and appear to be frozen stiff. Dolls like them were first shipped to America from Germany about 150 years ago. They got the name Frozen Charlotte from a song that was popular in the United States at the time. In the song, a lady named Charlotte rides in a sleigh with a boyfriend one wintry night. She refuses to wear a blanket because it will cover up her silk coat and scarf. When her boyfriend pulls the sleigh up to the dance, he finds that Charlotte has frozen to death. Frozen Charlotte dolls were usually only a few inches tall and made of china, rubber, metal, bisque, and even soap. They did not cost much, and many girls owned one. Sometimes a mother surprised her daughter by baking a Frozen Charlotte into her birthday cake.

FROZEN CHARLOTTES

From Germany, c. mid to late 19th century

GREEK DOLL

In ancient Greece, merchants sold clay dolls from stalls in outdoor markets. Some were brightly painted and had arms and legs that moved. If she'd finished helping her mother with spinning and weaving, a Greek girl might play with her doll in the courtyard. She'd dress her in a homemade tunic, and, if it was cool, fasten on a cloak. When the girl turned twelve or thirteen, a marriage was arranged, and she had to give up her dolls and toys. She went to a temple and, in a special ceremony, offered her playthings to the goddess Artemis (AR-tuh-miss). One poet wrote of a girl named Timarete (tim-ah-REH-tay), who said:

Maiden goddess, to you before her marriage, Timarete gives
Her cap, her tambourine, her favorite ball and as is proper, O Artemis,
her childhood toys, her dolls, her all.

From Greece, c. 350 BC

HARVEST DOLL

On the island of Bali, people eat rice with their meals three times a day, and they grow it for a living. They believe the grain is a gift from the goddess Dewi Sri (day-wee sree) who is beautiful, and loves fine music, dance, and art. To please Dewi Sri, many Balinese throw festivals throughout the year, and make her dolls. Before the rice is harvested, they weave strips of dried palm leaves into human shapes, which represent life. After the rice is reaped a great celebration takes place at a temple, where pairs of dolls are treated like newly married couples. They are adorned in white and yellow garments, entertained with music, and given offerings. Afterward, in a long procession, women carry them home on their heads. The dolls rest at last in the family rice granary on a wooden throne.

The native people of Alaska often spent long winter nights making dolls for their children. Mothers created them from seal skins stuffed with tundra grasses. Fathers carved little figures out of bone or walrus ivory. Their daughters sewed doll clothes with intricate patterns and designs, using the skins of mice, lemmings, and squirrels they possibly trapped themselves. Each stitch had to be sewn straight and tight, because in the Arctic, if your clothing tears, you might freeze. A girl might pretend she was a mother, tucking the doll in the hood of her parka to keep it warm. This exquisite set, which resembles an actual family, is outfitted in traditional garments. It was made by an Iñupiat (in-OOPEE-at) woman who used the sewing skills she learned as a girl, many winters ago.

IÑUPIAT DOLLS

From U.S., c. 1955

JUMEAU DOLL

In 1867, Emile Jumeau of France joined his father's doll company, and set out to produce the most elegant dolls on the market. A few years later, he created the Bebe Jumeau (bay-bay zjoo-MOH), a peach-faced doll with glass eyes that seemed human. Costumiers designed stylish fashions for them, using silk, lace, dyed feathers, and other materials. Thousands of Jumeau dolls were made for eager customers in Europe and America. A wealthy girl had a Bebe with accessories and a trunkful of outfits. She could change her doll's clothes several times a day, just as she changed her own. Her nanny would help her lace the tiny corsets and slip the ankle boots off and on. The girl might splash perfume on her doll from a miniature scent bottle, and imagine she was going to the opera.

From France, c. 1879–1880

KACHINA DOLL

The Hopi people of the southern United States believe in ancestor spirits that represent every part of life and nature. From late December to late July, the spirits—called Kachinas (kuh-CHEEN-uhs)—appear in the village to join the Hopi in their ceremonies and dances. The Kachinas help them pray for rain, good crops, and a life that's in balance. To teach children, especially girls, about the many different types of kachinas, the Hopi make dolls. Doll makers carve and whittle them from the roots of cottonwood trees. The figures are often painted with traditional symbols for plants, animals, the moon, stars, and rainbows. Some Kachinas are ogres who threaten to punish children if they misbehave. Nat a'aska (natah aashkah), the ogre pictured here, has a mouth so big, he can swallow them whole.

From U.S., 1943

LENCI DOLL

In the early twentieth century, in Torino, Italy, there lived an artist named Elena Scavini. Lots of factories in her town made felt and other cloth. Elena liked to create dolls out of the felt, pressing and molding it into little faces. She painted on their features, sewed on tufts of mohair on their heads, and decorated their clothes with the finest embroidery. When her husband went off to fight in a war, Elena decided to sell her dolls to make money. She made dozens of designs, including child dolls, character dolls, costume dolls, clowns, cowboys, and Indians. She named them "Lenci" (LEHN-chee), the Italian nickname for Elena. Lenci dolls were like works of art, and they were expensive. A mother might choose to buy one for decoration, rather than giving it as a toy. Her daughter could only gaze at the doll in its ruffled skirts, posed carefully on a shelf.

In the late nineteenth century, an artist named Sergei Malyutin (SEHR-gay mall-YOO-tin) saw a set of Japanese nesting dolls in a Moscow toy workshop. It may have reminded him of the Russian legend of the mother goddess Jumala, a golden statue that contained three figures, one inside the other. Malyutin asked his friend, an expert woodcarver, to carve a set. His friend made eight dolls by hollowing and shaping the soft wood of a linden tree. Malyutin painted an infant, a boy, and six girls, wearing babushkas, or handkerchiefs, on their heads. Soon other craftsmen were making their own versions of the dolls, known as matryoshkas (mah-tree-USH-kuhs). The most common numbers in a set are four to six, but the largest can include seventy. Matryoshkas are popular souvenirs, and many Russians keep them in their homes. Boys and girls like to sit on the floor and take each one apart, until they reach the teeniest—sometimes a baby no bigger than a grain of rice!

MATRYOSHKAS

NINA

In 1863, the United States was in the middle of a civil war. The North tried to prevent the South from getting food, weapons, medicine, and other supplies. Southerners devised clever ways to sneak items in from across the border. Women hid pistols in their bustle skirts. Messages were tucked in hairdos and hambones. And it's believed that dolls like this one—named Nina by her owner—were used for smuggling too. Their hollow papier-mâché heads could store secret cargo. In the arms of young ladies, they would not attract attention. Nina belonged to the niece of a major general from Tennessee. With an innocent look in her big blue eyes, she easily passed through enemy lines, carrying in her head several ounces of medicine for sick Confederate soldiers.

Possible German origin, c. mid 19th century

OZARK DOLLS

The pioneers learned from the Native Americans how to make dolls with dried apples. Later on, women in the Ozarks and other mountain areas crafted these applehead dolls to make extra money. Besides fruit, all they needed were sticks and cornhusks for bodies, scraps from the ragbag for clothes, and perhaps some paint for the cheeks. In fall or winter, a girl and her grandma would pick through a basket of large, juicy apples. They might decide that the squat, round one would make a good old woman. Her grandma would slit a smile, bore out holes for the eyes, and fashion a nose. The next day the apple meat was like spongy flesh that could be pinched and squeezed into a face. Over the next few weeks, they'd watch the doll to see what expression she'd make. You never knew which way the wrinkles would fall.

From U.S., c. 1950s

26

From Poland, c. mid 20th century to present

In 1287, Tartar warriors raged through Poland on their horses, burning villages and taking lives. In one legend, they tried to enter the city of Krakow, but were beaten back by a group of boatmen on the Vistula River. After the victory, one of the raftsmen slipped into the clothes of the enemy chief and rode through town on his steed. Today the Poles make brightly clothed wooden dolls of this brave man, called Lajkonik (lie-cone-eek), meaning "Little Horse." Fathers buy them for their children at the Pageant of Lajkonik, held the eighth Thursday after Easter. During the parade, Poles dressed like noblemen, villagers, and Tartar warriors wind their way from Wawel Castle to the market square. Then Lajkonik, dressed in his finery, comes galloping through. With a touch of his baton, he brings people good luck.

POLISH DOLL

Wooden dolls made in England two to three hundred years ago are known as Queen Annes, but they looked nothing like her royal majesty. The queen lived for part of the time during which the dolls were popular. Furniture makers gave these little lords and ladies large oval heads, slender waists, and long-fingered hands shaped like forks. The dolls wore tiny wigs made of human hair and handsome garments cut from satins and brocades. Because fabric was expensive, the outfits were sometimes sewn from curtain and upholstery trimmings. Queen Anne dolls were bought for the daughters of noble-men, landed gentry, and wealthy merchants. Aristocratic girls spent most of their day learning how to run the household, to sit and walk properly, to dance and play the harpsichord. Sitting in a drawing room full of relatives at teatime, a girl possibly looked forward to playing alone with her doll. She'd sit the young lady on her lap, take her forked hands, and whisper secrets.

QUEEN ANNE DOLL

RAMAKIEN DOLLS

One of the most well-known stories in Thailand is the Ramakien (rah-mah-KEE-yen). In the ancient tale, the evil ogre Ravana captures the wife of the noble Prince Rama from his forest home. With the help of a monkey king, Rama goes to war with the demon and rescues the princess. The Thais stage elegant ballets about the Ramakien, performed on splendid sets to singing and orchestral music. They also make dolls that look like the characters. The dolls model like graceful dancers, and wear costumes woven with metallic thread, gleaming with rhinestones and seed beads. Many Thais decorate their homes with Ramakien dolls. Perhaps a boy will pose like his monkey king or masked demon dancer, then break into a dance all of his own.

From Thailand, c. mid 20th century

SIOUX DOLL

The Sioux Indians of the northern plains of the United States cherished their children. They shielded them during warfare, fed them first when food was scarce, and told them stories of their ancestors. Mothers and grandmothers made buckskin dolls for young ones. When Sioux girls made doll clothes and accessories, they had a chance to practice their beadwork. They enjoyed playing camp with their dolls, using miniature tipis, gopher and squirrel skin rugs, and grass for food. Sometimes, young boys attacked with little warriors on toy ponies. As the years passed, the girls would outgrow their childhood possessions, but many held on to their favorite dolls.

From U.S., c. 1890

Of all the dolls created in American homes in the last century, those made of cloth were perhaps the most treasured. Stuffed with bran, straw, or sawdust, they were soft and cuddly. If their faces tore, they could be stitched up again. In the South, African Americans, forced to work as slaves, sewed cloth dolls for the girls they took care of. Dolls that had a different head at each end and a reversible skirt at the waist were called Topsy Turvies. Later these dolls were made for children throughout the country, often depicting characters from stories. One type showed Topsy and Eva, two girls from the novel *Uncle Tom's Cabin*. In the book, Topsy is a slave befriended by her master's daughter, Eva. In reality, girls like Topsy and Eva were often close companions. A cotton grower's daughter and her servant may have played under the orange trees with a Topsy Turvy, a black doll and white doll bound together like their lives.

TOPSY TURVY DOLL

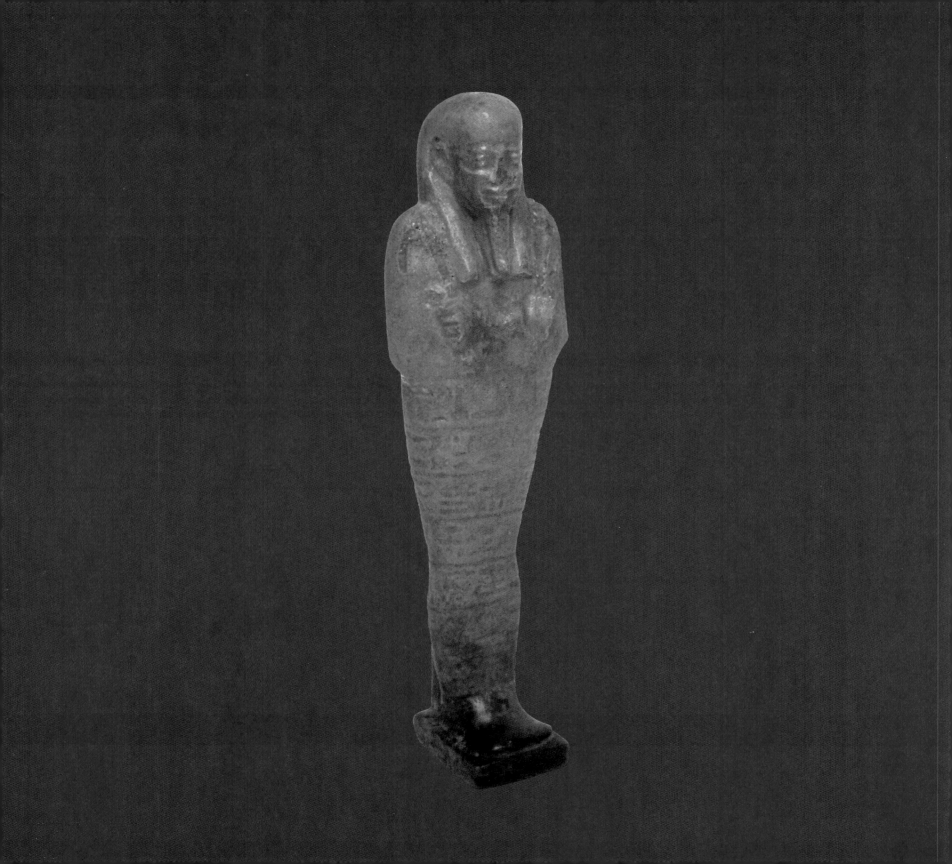

USHABTI

The ancient Egyptians believed that after death they lived forever in an afterworld that was just like Egypt. They were buried with everything they'd need there—food, clothes, furniture, cosmetics, hunting gear, and games. Egyptians made small dolls called Ushabtis (you-SHAHB-tees), which means "answerers." It was believed that if the God Osiris asked the dead man or woman to plough the fields, cook, make music, or do other chores in the afterworld, the Ushabtis would magically do the work. The dolls were inscribed with hieroglyphics that told the person's name, his rank in life, and the good deeds he'd done. The more distinguished the person, the more ushabtis he took with him. Some tombs had as many as 401—one servant for every day of the year, plus a boss for every week (the Egyptian weeks were ten days long). The tomb of King Seti I (1303–1290 B.C.) was packed with seven hundred of these little helpers, ready to spring to life in the hereafter.

From Egypt, c. 1000–500 B.C.

On the island of Haiti, most people worship Vodou spirits called loas (lwahs). Haitians ask the loa for help with their problems, using objects like sequinned bottles, jars wrapped in butcher string, and dolls. A woman who wants to recapture the love of an old boyfriend might seek help from a Vodou priestess. Together they'll make a cloth doll filled with magical ingredients. The priestess sprinkles in special herbs that work like magnets to attract people. As she stitches up the doll, the priestess might instruct the woman to concentrate on reclaiming the man she loves. A note is written to a spirit in a secret language, then attached to the doll. Afterward, the woman carries the little figure to a crossroads or cemetery, a holy place. The doll is left there in the hopes a spirit will answer the message pinned on its chest.

VODOU DOLLS

From Haiti, c. 1935

North American pioneers thought twice before throwing anything away. They usually lived miles away from shops and often didn't have the money to spend there. Women stored old buttons, bottles, clothespins, and other items. Chicken or turkey breastbones were saved after Sunday dinner, but not always for making wishes. Many mothers and children created wishbone dolls. A girl attached a piece of cork, putty, or melted sealing wax for the head, and used lanks of thread for hair. To make a dress, she might find a scrap of buckskin or some mattress ticking. While she stitched a bonnet from a bit of muslin, she might be thinking of a friend she missed. She'd give the wishbone doll to her in winter, when school started.

WISHBONE DOLLS

XMAS DOLLS

In November, hundreds of little clay shepherds, angels, and other figures appear in marketplaces throughout Mexico. They are molded and hand-painted in small workshops throughout the year. Families buy these colorful dolls, which they call *nacimientos* (nah-see-mee-EN-toes), for Nativity scenes they create in their homes. In the days before Christmas, many Mexicans set up wooden shelters which may be surrounded by paper-bag mountains and tinfoil rivers. The scene may be small enough to fit under a tree, or it may be as large as the room. Children are not allowed to play with the Nativity dolls, but they may help pose them. Possibly a child will take the baby out of the wrapper, and give it a kiss, before he sets it between Mary and Joseph.

From Mexico, c. 1960

The native people of the Andes have small mountain farms where they grow potatoes and other vegetables. While watching their herds of llamas or sheep, the women spin yarn. In one hand they hold a stick of unspun wool, and with the other they pull thread so it spools around a weighted spindle, often a stone or carrot. The women weave and knit their own clothes from this yarn, and some also make dolls to sell. The knitted dolls wear hats, vests, scarves, and skirts in the designs of the village they come from. In their arms may be musical instruments, llamas, babies, or even spinning equipment. A young child might persuade her mother to let her keep a doll rather than sell it in the marketplace. At night, lying on her straw mattress, she may sing to it until she falls asleep.

YARN DOLLS

From Peru, c. 1960

ZULU DOLL

When Zulu boys of South Africa tired of their clay cattle, and girls were past the age of playing with clay dolls, they began to think about getting married. Years ago, a young girl asked the leader of unmarried girls if she could court a boy she fancied. It was not acceptable for her to tell the young man her feelings. First, she acted grumpy when he was around. Next, she handed him a doll, made of beads tightly wound around a roll of cloth. She told the boy her doll's name. He wore it on a string over his shoulder, or hung it in his grass hut, perhaps with other dolls that were offered to him. If she was his favorite, the two would later marry. Someday, stringing beads alongside her daughter, the young woman might tell the story of her courtship and the doll, who was a messenger of love.

From South Africa, c. mid 20th century

U.S. (IÑUPIAT)

U.S. (SIOUX)

U.S. (NINA)

U.S. (KACHINA)

U.S. (OZARK)

U.S. (CORN, TOPSY TURVY, WISHBONE)

Mexico (XMAS)

Haiti (VODOU)

Ecuador (BREAD)

Peru (YARN)

In the U.S., lines show where the Kachina, Iñupiat, and the Sioux dolls originate. Nina is of possible German origin. Wishbone, Corn, and Topsy Turvy dolls have been made throughout the U.S. Dolls with apple heads have been made in many regions as well, but the Ozark region is particularly known for them.

Pointer lines do not indicate specific spots within countries.

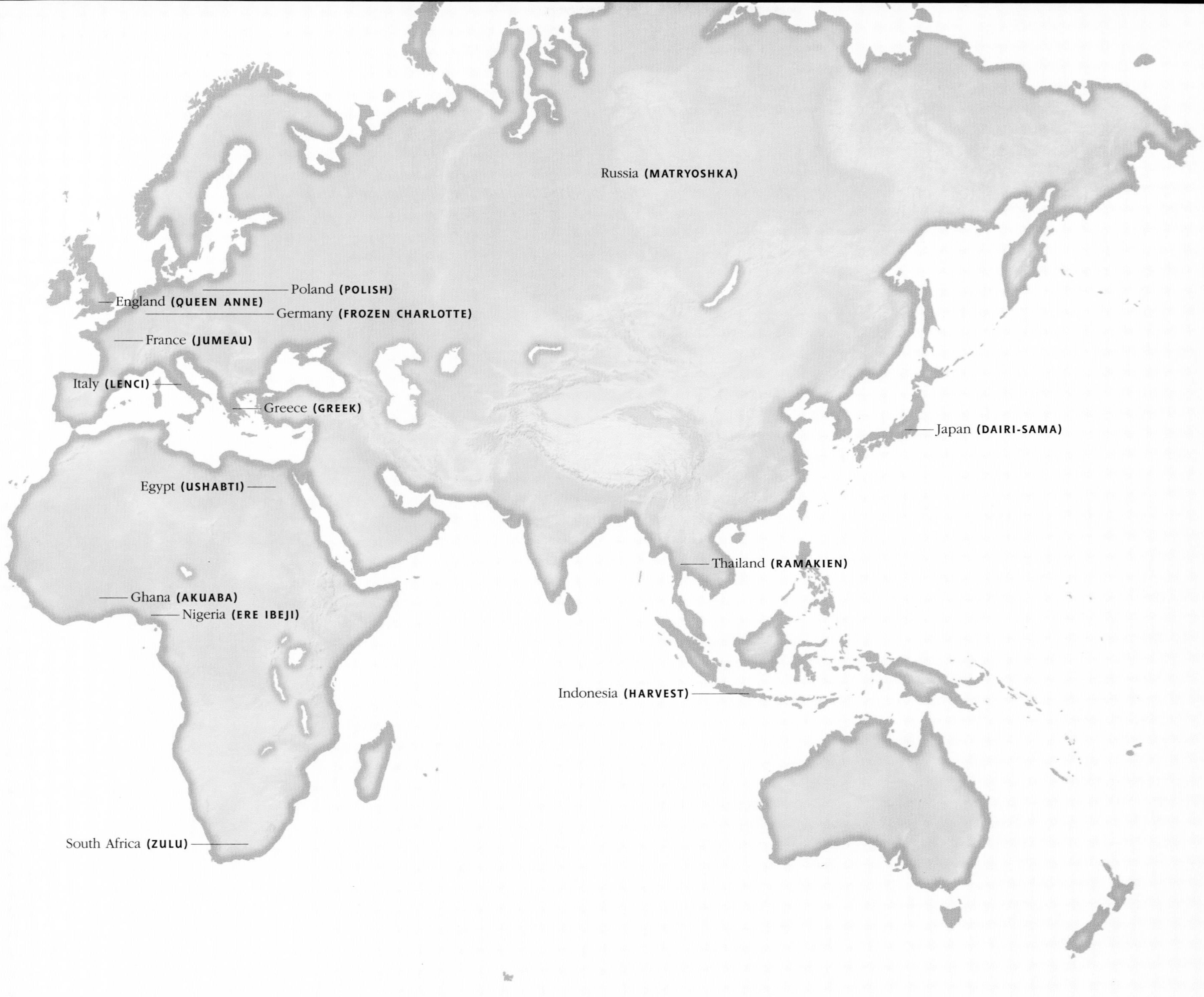

Russia **(MATRYOSHKA)**

Poland **(POLISH)**

England **(QUEEN ANNE)**

Germany **(FROZEN CHARLOTTE)**

France **(JUMEAU)**

Italy **(LENCI)**

Greece **(GREEK)**

Japan **(DAIRI-SAMA)**

Egypt **(USHABTI)**

Thailand **(RAMAKIEN)**

Ghana **(AKUABA)**

Nigeria **(ERE IBEJI)**

Indonesia **(HARVEST)**

South Africa **(ZULU)**

If you'd like to start your own doll collection, choose dolls that give you a special feeling when you look at them. They may be beautiful, their expressions may be funny, or they may remind you of a place you've seen. Collect whatever you like—bridal couples from India, costume dolls from Eastern Europe, or modern vinyl dolls from America. Everyone's tastes are different, and your collection will show the kind of person you are.

Dolls can be bought at antiques stores, specialty shops, import stores, flea markets, and garage sales. If you're serious about collecting, the best place to purchase dolls is at a doll show or convention from a reliable dealer. You don't necessarily need lots of money. Visit all the booths and tables to compare prices. Once you know the kind of doll you want to buy, choose the best example you can afford, and ask the dealer for all the information he or she has about it. Currently, the most inexpensive types are folk dolls from other countries. Look for finely crafted ones with appealing faces. If you're buying a modern manufactured doll, select one as close as possible to its original condition—not one that's been repaired or changed in any way.

Keep your doll on a shelf where you can take it down to play with, or just admire. But if you wish to preserve your dolls for the future, it's important to take precautions. You can buy the same boxes and tissue paper that museums use to store their objects. Check with your library to find out about a supplier. Remove brand-new dolls from their boxes, saving the box and all the accessories. Wrap the doll in the special paper (you can also use clean cotton sheets or washed unbleached muslin) before placing it in the box. Store it away from sunlight, moisture, and extreme heat or cold, checking for moths now and then.

Your collection may inspire you to become a doll maker. Look at your surroundings as an artist would, finding new ways to use ordinary objects. A plastic bottle could be the beginning of a body, a wooden spoon could be a head, strands of shredded paper could serve as hair. If you prefer, use traditional craft materials like clay, cloth, yarn, and pipe cleaners; or natural elements like shells, nuts, and twigs. Make a doll that looks silly, scary, or beautiful—or even like youself. If someone found your doll years from now, what would it tell them about you?

SELECTED BIBLIOGRAPHY

Bachmann, Manfred, and Claus Hansmann. *Dolls the Wide World Over*. New York: Crown Publishers, 1973.

Fox, Carl. *The Doll*. New York: Harry Abrams, 1972.

Goodfellow, Caroline. *The Ultimate Doll Book*. New York: Dorling Kindersley, 1993.

Hillier, Mary. *Pageant of Toys*. New York: Taplinger Publishing Co., 1966.

———. *Dolls and Doll Makers*. New York: Putnam, 1968.

Holz, Loretta. *The How-to Book of International Dolls*. New York: Crown Publishers, 1980.

Jolles, Frank. "Contemporary Zulu Dolls from Kwalatha." *African Arts,* Vol. 27, No. 2 (April 1994): 54–69.

Lavitt, Wendy. *American Folk Dolls*. New York: Alfred A. Knopf, 1982.

———. *Dolls*. New York: Alfred A. Knopf, 1983.

Lenz, Mary Jane. *The Stuff of Dreams: Native American Dolls*. New York: Museum of the American Indian, 1986.

Ramseyer, Urs. *The Art and Culture of Bali*. New York: Oxford University Press, 1977.

Sayer, Chloe. *Arts and Crafts of Mexico*. San Francisco: Chronicle Books, 1990.

Van Boehn, Max. *Dolls and Puppets*. New York: Cooper Square Publishers, 1966.

Museum Exhibit: "Isn't S/He a Doll?" Los Angeles: UCLA Fowler Museum of Cultural History, Nov. 17, 1996–Aug. 24, 1997.

ACKNOWLEDGMENTS

Special thanks to Diane Hamblin, former curator at the Wenham Museum, Massachusetts; Susan Hedrick, former curator at the Rosalie Whyel Museum of Doll Art, Bellevue, Washington; and Nancy Paine, curator at the Brooklyn Children's Museum, New York, for their patient answering of questions and generous sharing of knowledge. This book could not have been written without them. Thanks also to Elizabeth Cameron at the Los Angeles County Museum of Art, California; Terri Hudgins at the Museum of the Confederacy, Richmond, Virginia; Mary Jane Lenz at the National Museum of the American Indian, Smithsonian Institution, Suitland, Maryland; Doran Ross at the Fowler Museum of Cultural History, UCLA, Los Angeles; Kim Walters at the Southwest Museum, Los Angeles; Rebecca Rich-Wulfmeyer at the Museum of International Folk Art, Santa Fe, New Mexico; Professor Karen McCarthy Brown at Drew University, Madison, New Jersey; Yegis Naidu of the Natal Museum, Pietermaritzburg, South Africa; Elizabeth Koszarski-Skrabonja at the Kosciusko Foundation, New York; Professor Frank Jolles of the University of Natal, Pietermaritzburg, South Africa; Professor Raymond Scupin at Lindenwood University, St. Charles, Missouri; Jan Jordan at the American School of Classical Studies, Athens, Greece; the Consulate of Ecuador, Los Angeles; the Consulate of Japan, Los Angeles; and the former librarians at the Craft and Folk Art Museum, Los Angeles. I'm grateful also to John Darcy Noble, Glenn Russell, Heather Stockdale, Eve Boicourt, Basia Dziewanowska, Professor Aryati Hunter, Professor Thomas Hunter, and my mother, Bea Markel. For their advice and encouragement, I'm indebted to Ann Whitford Paul and Barbara Layman. These and many others were of great assistance.